**World
History
According
to College
Students**

NON

CAMPUS

MENTIS

Compiled by

Professor Anders Henriksson

Workman Publish

D1041725

To Youth,

whose imagination

lifts my spirits

Henriksson, Anders.
  Non campus mentis : world history according to college students/compiled by Professor Anders Henriksson.
    p. cm.
ISBN 0-7611-2274-5 (hc); 0-7611-2979-0 (pb)
  1. American wit and humor. 2. History—Humor. I. Title.

PN6231.B8 H46 2001
902'.07—dc21   2001026984

Pages 146–147, 148–149, 150: outline of map © by RMC, R.L. 01-S-60. www.randmcnally.com.

Workman books are available at special discounts when purchased in bulk for premiums and sales promotions as well as for fund-raising or educational use. Special editions or book excerpts can also be created to specification. For details, contact the Special Sales Director at the address below.

Workman Publishing Company, Inc.
708 Broadway
New York, NY 10003-9555
www.workman.com

Printed in the United States of America

First paperback printing: March 2003

10 9 8 7 6 5 4 3 2 1

Photo credits: All text photographs are from Bettmann/CORBIS except for the following: AUSTRIAN ARCHIVE: p. 112. THE BRIDGEMAN ART LIBRARY: p. 22 (Museuo Nattzionale di Tarquinia); p. 48 (John Carter Brown Library, B.U.); pp. 72 (top), 91 (private collection); p. 94 (Royal Geographical Society, London). CHRISTIES IMAGES: p. 63. CORBIS: pp. 44, 55, 58 (left) (Archivo Iconografico); pp. 57, 67, 103 (Christel Geretenberg); p. 124 (Flip Schulke); p. 15 (Francis Mayer); pp. 5, 27 (Gianni Dagli Orti); p. 58 (right) (Historical Picture Archive); pp. 96, 97, 102, 112, 118 (Hulton-Deutsch); pp. 82, 105 (top) (Leonard de Selva); p. 21 (Michael Maslan Historic Photographs); p. 11 (National Gallery Collection); p. 135 (bottom) (Owen Franken); p. 37 (Sakamoto Photo Research Lab); p. 122 (Yavegeny Khaidei). GRANGER COLLECTION: pp. 29, 50. MAPS.COM: p. 132. MARY EVANS PICTURE LIBRARY: p. 3. NASA: p. 137. NATIONAL ARCHIVES: p. 8. NEW YORK PUBLIC LIBRARY: pp. 10, 19, 34, 52, 65, 72 (bottom). PHOTOFEST: p. 93 (top). WIDE WORLD PHOTOS: pp. 152–153.

Acknowledgments

This book has been a collaborative effort. The real authors, of course, are probably best served by anonymity. I do, however, wish to thank those colleagues at Shepherd College and at numerous other learned institutions who have contributed work of their own students, especially James Greenlee at the Memorial University of Newfoundland, whose *Cretinalia Historica,* compiled from final exams, has been a treasure trove of insight into the past. Thanks also to Professor Arthur Preisinger, who kindly permitted me to mine his extensive collection of student gems.

I am also grateful to everyone who helped transform my raw material into publishable form. It was a delight to work with Steve Lagerfeld and *The Wilson Quarterly,* which published portions of this material in 1983 and in 2000. I am indebted to my agent, Daniel Greenberg, whose wise counsel and enthusiastic initiative brought this project to fruition, and my editor Ruth Sullivan, whose creative insight and sense of humor is present on every page. No small credit goes to my wife, Ann, whose encouragement and support have been a constant.

CONTENTS

INTRODUCTION

History is a work in progress. Every generation has to make sense of the past for itself. The facts may stay the same, but the work of interpretation goes on and on. This brief text glimpses at the cutting edge of this process. Culled from term papers and bluebook exams written by college and university students, it is an authentic voice of youth. Their work represents a refreshing and daring reappraisal of how we came to be who we are.

I have taken the liberty of weaving their sentences into a more-or-less coherent fabric, but the words belong to them. The spelling may be avant-garde and the logic experimental, but no one can fault these young scholars for lack of creativity. At its best, *Non Campus Mentis* (a typical student mishearing of *non compos mentis*) illustrates the ingenious and often comic ways we all attempt to make sense of information we can't understand because we have no context or frame of reference for it.

One source for this text has been the work of my own students, gleaned over nearly three decades from papers submitted to me at Shepherd College, a four-year West Virginia state college about ninety minutes from Washington, D.C., and at three leading Canadian research universities—Alberta, McMaster, and Toronto. The bulk of the raw material has been harvested by my colleagues from student prose at more than two dozen additional colleges and universities, among them some of the most selective and academically renowned institutions in the United States and Canada.

Sigmund Freud was a shrink who came up with sex reasoning.

Chapter 1
THE HISTORIAN'S TASK:
Hindsight into the Future

History, a record of things left behind by past generations, started in 1815. Thus we should try to view historical times as the behind of the present. This gives incite into the anals of the past.

Many things in history are inevitable when somebody does something. If we learn about the coarse of events we can prevent ourselves from doing it again. History, as we know, is always bias, because human beings have to be studied by other human beings, not by independent observers of another species.

Freud opened the door to people understanding what it is to open your own mind instead of having the thought that others had already.

From the secondary sources we are given hindsight into the future. **Hindsight, after all, is caused by a lack of foresight.** Another useful method to achieve this and other perspectives is through textual decomposition. Literature can open valuable windows into the past if the reader is careful to pluck bites of reality from the author's figlets of imagination.

My brain is on hold, so I can't remember much. So without further adieu, let's get to the research!

Chapter 2

THE DAWN OF TIME:
The Stoned Age

Bible legend states that the trouble started after Eve ate the Golden Apple of Discord. This was the forbidding fruit. An angry God sent his wraith. Man fell from the space of grace. It was mostly downhill skiing from there.

Prehistory, a subject mainly studied by anthroapologists, was prior to the year 1500. When animals were not available the people ate nuts and barrys. Social division of labour began

PReHiSTORiCLe PeOPLe spent aLL day banging ROCkS TOgeTHeR so that they couLd Find something To eat. this was the Stoned Age.

when a tribe would split into hunters and togetherers. Crow Magnum man had a special infinity for this. Advances were most common during the inter-galactic periods.

Early agriculture was known as "scratch and burn." One origin of religion was worry about crops or fertility, where a person prayed to certain gods so that he or she could give birth.

We feel fortunate not to have to live threw these times.

Chapter 3
THE MISTS OF ANTIQUITY:
The Joy of Flooding

Civilization woozed out of the Nile about 300,000 years ago. The Nile was a river that had some water in it. Every year it would flood and irritate the land. This tended to make the people nervous.

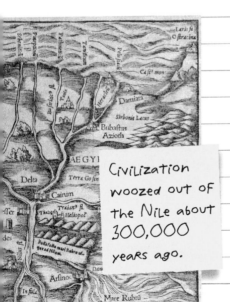

Civilization woozed out of the Nile about 300,000 years ago.

There was Upper Egypt and Lower Egypt. Lower Egypt was actually farther up than Upper Egypt, which was, of course, lower down than the upper part.

This is why we learn geography as a factor in history.

Rulers were entitled Faroes. A famed one was King Toot. It was a special custom among them not to marry their wives.

The pyramids were large square triangles built in the desert. O'Cyrus, a god who lived in a piramid, would give you the afterlife if your sole was on straight.

Members of the upper class were able to live posthumorusly through the art and facts buried with them. Eventually the Egyptians drowned in the desert.

Mesapatamia was squigged in a valley near the Eucaliptus river. Flooding was erotic.

Babylon was similar to Egypt because of the differences they had apart from each other. Egypt, for example, had only Egyptians, but Babylon had Summarians, Acadians, and Canadians, to name just a few.

The Sumerian culture, which was oldest, began about 3,500 years before Christmas.

People were allowed democratic freedoms like taking an eye for an eye and a tooth for a tooth.

King Nebodresser lived in a hanging garden to please his Hutterite wife.

Hammurabi was a lawyer who lived from 1600 B.C. to 1200 B.C.

The Babylonians honored their gods by building pyramids in the shape of zeplins.

The Assyrian program of exterminating various ethnic groups generally failed to promote cultural diversity. Founder of the Persian Empire was Medea. Persian kings kept power by dividing their land into providences administrated by sandtraps friendly to the king.

Zorroastrologism was founded by Zorro. This was a duelist religion.

The three gods were "Good," "Bad," and "Indifferent." These beliefs later resurfaced among the Manatees.

The history of the Jewish people begins with Abraham, Issac, and their twelve children. Judyism was the first monolithic religion. It had one big God named "Yahoo." Old Testament profits include Moses, Amy, and Confucius, who believed in Fidel Piety. (One of the only reasons Confucius was born was because of a Chinese tradition.)

Moses was told by Jesus Christ to lead the people out of Egypt into the Sahaira Desert. The Book of Exodus describes this trip and the amazing things that happened on it, including the Ten Commandments, various special effects, and the building of the Suez Canal.

Judyism had one big God named "Yahoo."

Forty centuries later they arrived in Canada. This was the promise land of milk and chocolate. Noah's ark came to its end near Mt. Arafat. David was a fictional character in the Bible who fought with Gilgamesh while wearing a sling. He pleased the people and saved them from attacks by the Philipines.

Chapter 4

THE CLASSICAL AGE:
Thucydides Meets the Mouse of History

The Trojan War Raged between the Greeks and the Tories.

Helen of Troy launched a thousand ships with her face. The Trojan War raged between the Greeks and the Tories. The Greeks finally won because they had wooden horses, while the Trojans were only able to fight with their feet.

Greek semen ruled the Agean. We know about this thanks to Homer's story about Ulysees Grant and Iliad, the painful wife he left behind.

- **Another myth with a message was Jason's hunt for the Golden Fleas.**
- **Thesis killed the Minosaur.**
- **King Minoose became Head Cretin.**

The Classical Age flashed onto the screen. Athens, Sparta, and Pluto were Greek city states. Some were Oglearchies. Athens was a democracy resulting from the reforms of Colon and Percales.

The Parthenonon was Pericles' greatest erection.

Sparta demanded loyalty, military service, and obscurity from its citizens.

Men during this period were usually about thirty years old and women only twelve or thirteen.

Arranged marriages required women to accept a kind of *mate accompli*. King Xerox of Persia invaded Greace, but fell off short at the battle of Thermosalami. Philip of Mastodon captured Greece and then was killed in a family sprawl.

Alexander the Great conquered Persia, Egypt, and Japan. Sadly, he died with no hairs.

Religion was polyphonic. Featured were gods such as Herod, Mars, and Juice. Persepolis was god of vegtables. Souls were believed to spend the "here, there and after" in Ethiopia.

The Greeks were important at culture and science. Many Greek ideas have noodled down through history and still influense us here today.

Thucydides was a noted historian who collected facts objectively and saw himself as responsible only to Clio, the Greek Mouse of History.

The scientific method came into use when the Greeks learned never to take things for granite when solving a problem.

- **The Atomists discovered the concept E=MC2.**
- **The Sophists justified themselves by changing relatives whenever this needed to be done.**

These pre-Socratics lived long before Plato and were not decisively influenced by his work.

Socrates was accused of sophmorism and sentenced to die of hemroyds.

Plato invented reality. He was teacher to Harris Tottle, author of *The Republicans.* Lust was a must for the Epicureans. Others were the Vegetarians and the Synthetics, who said, *"If you can't play with it, why bother?"*

Scrophicles developed these ideas in the play *Antipode* about a young girl, her boyfriend, and her misfunctional family.

- **U. Clid proved that there is more than one side to every plain.**
- **Pythagasaurus fathered the triangle.**
- **Archimedes made the first steamboat and power drill.**

The Ancient Greeks founded the Olympics in about 1896.

Chapter 5
THE GRANDEUR THAT WAS ROME:
Me Too, Brutus!

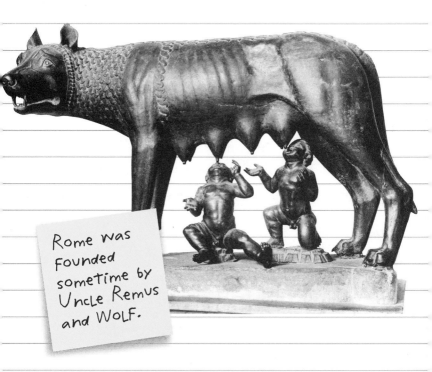

Rome was
founded
sometime by
Uncle Remus
and WOLF.

Society was inedibly stamped
with class conflict. Elitists practised
various snubberies over the masses.

Roman upperclassmen demanded to be known as Patricia. Senators wore purple tubas as a sign of respect. Around the 120s B.C. the Gretzky brothers failed to stop these and other injustices.

Slaves led existances of long and ornery work. Spartacus led a slave revolt and later was in a movie about this. The Roman republic was bothered by intestinal wars.

Hannabelle crossed the Alps with a herd of eliphants and thus invaded Africa. After they defeated Carthage the Romans brutaly salted the people and razored the city. Scipio was called "Africanus" because he served in Spain. One of Rome's early victories came against the Samsonites.

Cesar was assinated on the Yikes of March.

Cesar inspired his men by stating, **"I came, I saw, I went."**

When he was assinated, he is reported to have said, **"Me too, Brutus!"**

After many turmoilic events, including Anthony's elusive affair with Cleopatra, the shrewd Octavian grabbed hold of the Empire. He kept the people happy by giving them breaded circuses.

Augustus (a.k.a. Octagenarian) founded the Roman Catholic Empire and punished those involved in sibilancy and adultry. The symbol of his authority was the cross. He put it everywhere. Augustus did have to leave the Empire due to his death.

The Romans had smaller, more practical brains than the Greeks. Pagan Roman philosophers included Cicero, Marcus Aorta, and St. Jerome. Stoicism is the belief that you should get through life by baring your troubles. This is shown in the *Medications* of Marcus Aurelius.

The warmth and friendship of the mystery cults attracted many, who came to feel better through dancing and mutilation. Certain cultists followed Diane Isis, the godess of whine.

Roman girls who did not marry could become Vestigal Virgins, a group of women who were dedicated to burning the internal flame.

Temple of the Vestigal Virgins

Romans persecuted Christians by Lionizing them.

Chapter 6

THE RISE OF CHRISTIANITY AND THE FALL OF ROME:
The Immaculate Contraption

Christianity was just another mystery cult until Jesus was born. The mother of Jesus was Mary, who was different from other women because of her immaculate contraption.

Mary and Joseph went from inn to inn trying to find a place for Jesus to be born, but they were refused everywhere because they were Jewish.

Eventually Christian started the new religion with sayings like, ***"The mice shall inherit the earth."*** Later Christians fortunately abandoned this idea.

Romans persacuted Christians by lionizing them in public stadiums. Among the things that helped Christianity grow was the promise of an eternal afterword.

- **St. Augustine became a pillar in the Catholic church.**
- **St. Jerome refused to believe in sex.**
- **The Arians denied the holy triangle.**
- **Pope Gregory the Great had to confront the Gnosts.**
- **St. Benedict gave his monks a set of punitive rules to enjoy.**

St. Jero

Christianity finally became official after the Emperor Constantine's famous Decree of Consternation. Constantine became a Christian himself after being persued by a neon cross on the battlefield. The entire city of Constantinople rose up with a tremendous ejaculation every time the emperor came.

Many of the theories about the fall of the Roman Empire were totally not possible, and some of them were. This included more than enough religion, too much slavery, not enough water, and smoking from lead pipes.

A tidul wave of Goths, Hungs, Zulus, and others impacted Rome.

Athena the Hun

Athena the Hun rampaged the Balkans as far as France, where he plumaged and tortured people of the villages he captured.

Society was crumpity. Neo-Platonists celebrated the joys of self-abuse.

When they finally got to Italy, the Australian Goths were tired of plungering and needed to rest. Italy was ruled by the Visible Goths, while France and Spain were ruled by the Invisible Goths.

A German soldier put Rome in a sack.

During the Dark Ages it was mostly dark.

Chapter 7

THE FEUDAL WORLD:
The Rise of the Manurial System

Society was arranged like a tree, with your nobels in the upper twigs and your pesants grubbing around the roots.

It is unfortunate that we do not have a medivel European laid out on a table before us, ready for dissection. Society was arranged like a tree, with your nobels in the upper twigs and your pesants grubbing around the roots. This was known as the

manurial system where land was
passed through fathers to sons by
primogenuflecture. To some degree
rulers diluted people into thinking
that this was a religious operation.

During the Middle Ages everyone
was middle aged. People lived in or
near the soil. Most were kept busy
sewing the crops. Surfs were dentured
and bonded to the ground. In times
of crisis the serfs would seek refuse
in the lord's castle.

**Medieval people were violent.
Murder during this period was
nothing. Everybody killed someone.**

Power belonged to a patriarchy empowering all genders except the female. Nuns, for example, were generally women. In the early part of the Middle Ages female nuns were free to commit random acts of contrition and redemption. Later they were forcibly enclustered in harems.

Hildegard of Bingen, whose parents were informed by a cow that she should be a nun, was later a musical composer, herbiologist, and abyss.

Hildegard frequently used her mystical visions to put dents in the patriarch.

Gratian, the leading Middle Evil authority on women, was born around 1140 B.C. A position as lady-in-mating helped a young girl's chances for a marriage useful to her family. Wives of noblemen held certain power tools although they were branded with his symbol.

The Right of the First night Let Lords spend the wedding night with the bride instead of the husband.

Chapter 8

CHURCH AND STATE IN MEDIEVAL EUROPE:
Vacant Bishop Bricks

Monks simply preyed by day and played by night.

Medeval monarchy was futile. Charlemagne used the "missi dominici" (Latin for "missiles of the king") to inflict government on his people.

The Wholely Roman Empire amazed many when it was found in Germany. The Kievan state was wreaked by civil war because Prince Vladimir had more sons than needed, a result of several wives and many columbines.

Around the year 1000 people were afraid that an acropolis was lurking around the corner.

In 1066 England was overrun by Norman the Conqueror. England's Henry II acquired new parts by marrying Ellenor of Equine.

Richard the Loined Heart became highly popular as his life was promoted by the matadors who formed a circle around his mother.

Richard the Loined Heart

Church and state were co-operatic.
Mideval Europeans attended the Latin
church for as yet there were no Christians.

The power of the Popes was
based on the Holy Sea. Innocent III
authored Canine Law to regulate
church operations.

Unoccupied Bishop Bricks could
be cause for problems. The Bishop
Brick of Melon, for example, became
vacant in 1075.

Gregory VII's letter to Henry IV
was an example of the church's
struggle against secular encrouchment.
Henry won this debate by displaying
himself in the snow on Christmas
morning. After his death the

English Church used Thomas Becket as a mortar.

The power of the church was based on soul control of the sacer mints. Highly prized were remnants of saints and holy ones. Pentecost was accustomed as a big feast of the Holy Spirit flying overhead.

Metrification of the flesh was often an important ritual. At times people mortifed themselves with cheese cloth and ashes in order to display their faith.

The Mortardom of St. Thomas

Monks were assigned to monkeries, where they were suppose to live as nuns. Many, however, simply preyed by day and played by night. Fryers were required to take a vow of pottery.

If you disagreed with the church you were accused of hear say and treated to excomunication. An important example of this was the Catheter movement in southern France. Members of this group were feared as possibly lethal.

Medieval builders gave God his usual chair in the church roof. In a Romanesque church the stone roof is held up by a system of peers. The usual design was a long knave split by a crosshair. Without the discovery of the flying buttock it would have been an impossible job to build the Gothic cathedral.

The flying buttock

The Hundred Years War (1320–1600) was fought over English holidays in France. The kingdom was left weak and venerable from these attacks. Royal power was reduced to a small area around the Eel of France.

The crusades enlarged opportunities for travel. These were a series of military expaditions made by Christians seeking to free the holy land (the "Home Town" of Christ).

- **The Mongrels advanced into Syria and Egypt in 1260.**
- **Harun Al-Rashid rose to Calico of the Islams.**
- **Jihad became a Swahili god.**
- **The Turks enjoyed the peek of power.**
- **Margo Polo visited Kukla Kahn, who rained in China at the time.**

Qin Shihuangdi did away with Confusionism. He is also seen as a megalomaniac who had six thousand soldiers made out of pottery to protect him from the afterlife. Russia was run over by Batu Cohen and crushed under the Mongol yolk.

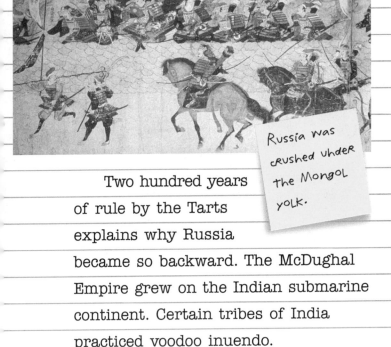

Russia was cRushed uhdeR the MongoL yoLk.

Two hundred years of rule by the Tarts explains why Russia became so backward. The McDughal Empire grew on the Indian submarine continent. Certain tribes of India practiced voodoo inuendo.

The bubonic plague is a social disease in the sense that it can be transmitted by intercourse and other etceteras.

Victims of the Black Death grew boobs on their necks.

Chapter 9

THE WANING OF THE MIDDLE AGES:
A Plague of Boobs

New things loamed on the horizon.

- **In the 1400 hundreds most Englishmen were perpendicular.**
- **A class of yeowls arose.**
- **Revolters ran apluck.**
- **Women were nowhere to be found.**
- **Martin Guerre, a French pesent, did not even seem to care if his wife produced a hare.**

After a revival of infantile commerce slowly creeped into Europe, merchants appeared. Some were sitters and some were drifters. They roamed from town to town exposing themselves and organized big fairies in the countryside.

Escaped peseants could be free if they went to a city and hid there for a hundred years and a day.

New weapons forced the nobels to deride from their horses. The longbow, for example, was a kind of bow and arrow only more painful. Knights now had to carry armoured plates into battle.

Jousting with Longbow

Castles became more elaborate
with thick walls, moats, and towers
topped by rows of
crustaceans.

Kings resented
Popal authority. This
caused the so-called
Divestiture
Controversy and led
to the Bolivian
Captivity of the
Church. The French
king moved the
Popes to Arizona
where he could keep
an eye on them.

Monks failed to practice morals between their prayers. The Council of Constance failed to solve this even though Constance herself tried very hard. Followers of Wyclif were known as Mallards.

John Huss refused to decant his ideas about the church and was therefore burned as a steak.

John Huss, burned as a steak

Finally, Europe caught the Black Death. The bubonic plague is a social disease in the sense that it can be transmitted by intercourse and other etceteras.

- **It was spread from port to port by inflected rats.**
- **It was then passed around by midgets.**
- **Victims of the Black Death grew boobs on their necks.**
- **Death rates exceeded one hundred percent in some towns.**

This was a time of stunned growth. The plague also helped the emergance of English as the national language of England, France, and Italy.

NICOL VS MACCHIAVELLI

Machiavelli, who was often unemployed, wrote The Prince to get a job with Richard Nixon.

Chapter 10
THE RENAISSANCE:
The Grits of Change

The Middle Ages slimpared to a halt.

- **The renasence bolted in from the blue.**
- **Life reeked with joy.**
- **Italy became robust, and more individuals felt the value of their human being.**
- **It became sheik to be educated.**

Italy, of course, was much closer to the rest of the world, thanks to northern Europe.

Thomas More put the capital "H" in Humanism. Erasmus wrote the *New Testament*. Chamber music was composed for groups of viles. Women, however, were required to display their art ominously.

Renaissance merchants were beautiful and almost lifelike. They enriched themselves by planting wool and selling it for clothing. They increased these profets by paying interest to people who borowed money from them. This produced even more grits for the mills of change.

Machiavelli, who was often unemployed, wrote *The Prince* to get a job with Richard Nixon.

Henry VIII divorced his original wife, who had become old and impregnable. Elizabeth I was eventually the daughter of Henry the Ate. Mother to Elizabeth was Ann Beau Lynne, wife of the moment to Henry VIII.

As queen, Elizabeth was the foremost monarch of the Elizabethan era. In 1588 she calmed her soldiers during a Spanish attack by assuring them that she shared a stomach with her father.

Charles V spent most of his reign aging.

Explorers went to look for trade roots. Ships were microscopically small and suffered bequalment if they could not make enough wind.

Ivan the Terrible started life as a child, a fact that troubled his later personality.

The invention of the sex tent helped to determine place and orientation at sea.

This was the beginning of Empire
when Europeans felt the need to
reach out and smack someone.

Man was determined to civilise
himself and his brothers, even if
heads had to roll!

Ferdinand and Isabella
conquered Granola, a part
of Spain now known as
Mexico and the Gulf States.

Magellan
circumsised
the glob.

Francis Drake was permitted
by Queen Elizabeth to sail the seas
and find illegal things to do with the
Spanish.

Columbus came to America to
install rule by dead white males over
the native peoples.

Cortez was leader of a little group of torriadors who subdued the inhabitants of New Mexico with great ease. Small box, which they brought with them, was killing the natives at a very quick rate. This bothered the Spanish little, for as Catholics they did not believe in God.

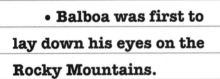

> The Vikings, of course, had already saled as far as Colorado, where several of their campsights can still be visited today.

- **Balboa was first to lay down his eyes on the Rocky Mountains.**
- **Dick Cavett was the first European to visit Newfoundland.**
- **Cabot discovered the Netherlands and codfish.**
- **Captain Cook found many continents while deliberately on exhibition and located the perfect navel spot near Africa's bottom.**

An angry Martin Luther nailed ninety-five theocrats to a church door.

Chapter 11

THE REFORMATION:
The Perils of Pope Clementine

The Reformnation happened
when German nobles resented the
idea that tithes were going to Papal
France or the Pope thus enriching
Catholic coiffures.

The growing disgust with the
mass amount of wealth the church
hoards became a definitive bone with
the people.

Traditions had become oppressive
so they too were crushed in the
wake of man's quest for ressurection
above the not-just-social beast he had
become.

The Catholic church sold indulgences as a form of remission control. Luthar was into reorientation mutation. An angry Martin Luther nailed ninety-five theocrats to a church door. The Pope's response was to declare Luther hereditary.

Lutherans began to meet in little churches with large morals painted on their walls. Martin Luther King stood for the priesthood of all relievers.

Calvin was born a gen-eration after Luther and is seen as one of Luther's greatest predecessors. He accepted all Luther's ideas except that of birth.

John Calvin Klein translated the Bible into American so the people of Geneva could read it.

- **Calvinists were the only ones who believed in pre-detonation. It is not surprising that their preaching consisted mainly of dogmatic explosions.**

- **Most Prodesants objected to holy communication.**

- **Anabaptist services tended to be migratory.**

- **The Popes, of course, were usually Catholic.**

The highlite of the Catholic Reform was the Council of Trend, which decreed that if man did not believe in the birth of the earth he would go to Hell. Catholics insisted on transmigration. Believers were still required to perform pinnace after sin.

- **Pope Clementine was clueless.**
- **Ignatius Loyola founded the Jesuits and many colleges in the United States.**
- **Monks went right on seeing themselves as worms.**
- **The last Jesuit priest died in the 19th century.**

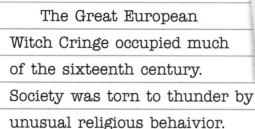

St. Teresa of Avila was a carmelized nun.

The Great European Witch Cringe occupied much of the sixteenth century. Society was torn to thunder by unusual religious behaivior.

Witch hunts erupted in countries such as Germany, England, Scotland, and Salem. The victim profile was older post-marsupial women unable to bare children. Those arrested were torchured until they told a story. The worst of this could be the rack or burning with hot porkers. Some unfortunate women were made to endure the public duckling stool.

After the refirmation were wars both foreign and infernal. Philip II later annoyed the Dutch by speaking to them in Spanish, a language he did not understand.

Philip II tried to force religious monotony on his empire.

If the Spanish could gain the Netherlands they would have a stronghold throughout northern Europe which would include their posetions in Italy, Burgangy, central Europe, and India thus serrounding France.

The religious war in France was known as the War of the Three Henrys, as it was fought between Henry III, Henry of Geese, and Francis II.

- **Henry Bourbon married Edict of Nantes and became King of France with the promise to reconstipate the country to Catholicism.**
- **The German Emperor's lower passage was blocked by the French.**
- **Not surprisingly, the English demanded special dissipation from the Pope.**
- **Henry VIII survived an assault from the Papal bull.**

Chapter 12

THE AGE OF ABSOLUTISM:
Musketeers and Round Ones

The Prussian army would surprise young men by grabbing them in unFair places.

Louise XIII attacked New Rochelle. Louis XIV became King of the Sun. He gave the people food and artillery. If he didn't like someone, he sent them to the gallows to row for the rest of their lives.

Royal absolutism thus became a progressive force, because it didn't put up with complainers. Vauban was the royal Minister of Flirtation.

The hiring of professional armies made aggression more controlled and intimate. The Prussian army, for example, would surprise young men by grabbing them in unfair places and sending them to Shanghigh. Gustav Adolf Hitler perched on the Swedish throan and looked droolingly at Germany.

- **The Thirty Years War began with the Defecation of Prague.**
- **Prague was capitol of Bulemia, where they always knew the emperor ahead of time.**
- **The Holy Omen Empire soon collapsed like a pack of cards.**

These good times ended when England suffered Civil War between the Musketeers and the Round Ones. Oliver Cromwell solved this and other problems by removing prominent things from people who disagreed with him. The Anglo-Dutch Trade Wars broke out because of trade and possibly not. Winston Churchill helped begin a New England colony.

King James Stuart Charles I was beheaded in 1649 and restored with his family several years later.

This was a time when the people could breed more easily. **Sex emerged from hiding and became very fashionable.** This extended until the secession of William Mary, who flew in from the Neverlands. We call this "Gloriana's Revolution of 1688."

East of the back of the beyond were the Russians, who knew nothing at all during this period. A factor in this was their use of the Kinetic alphabet. In Russia the 17th Century was known as the time of the bounding of the serfs.

Russian nobles wore clothes only to humour Peter the Great. Peter filled his cabinet with accidental people and built a new capital near the European boarder. Orthodox priests became government antennae. Catherine the Great rose to power only because her husband had been murdered by his clothiers for failure to incubate.

Catherine the Great became the Longest Female to rule Russia.

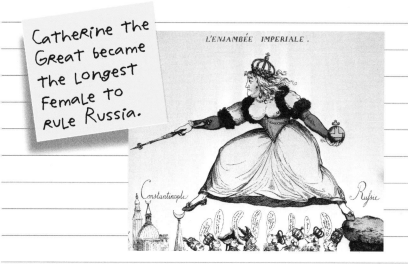

Charles III of Spain swooned for years on the bridge of extinction. The War of the Spanish Succession ended in a drawl. Peace was inforced by the Treaty of Uterus, which prevented the King of France from sitting personally on the Spanish thorn. The War of the Austrian Suspicion broke out soon after this. It had become very inevitable when Mother Theresa inherited the throne.

Frederick William the Electrode fought on both sides of several wars.

Chapter 13
THE ENLIGHTENMENT:
The Invention of the Newton

Deism was the belief that God made the world and then stepped on it.

There was an increase in climate during the eighteenth century. Agriculture fed more people as crop yields became lower. These were factors in the better times to come.

The Scientific Revolution developed a suppository of knowledge which greatly helped later generations. Copernicus showed that the solar system rotates around the earth. Galileo was condemned for following the Copernican theory and was forced by the Church to study mechanics for the rest of his life. Sir Issac Newton invented the newton.

- **It was the 18th century Enlightenment that contributed most to the 17th century.**
- **The Enlightenment was a reasonable time that seeped slowly into one of Europe's ears and then creeped out the other.**
- **Philosophy was based on falsies and this led to shaky foundations.**
- **When religion is put on a pestitule by the state people loose their passion for religion.**

The fundamental stake was one of religious toleration slightly confused with defeatism. Deism was the belief that God made the world and then stepped on it. In Deism God has no direct influence on daily life, but just watches like a movie, eating his candy and munching his popcorn.

Diderot became a famous encyclicalist. Voltare wrote a book called *Candy* that got him into trouble with Frederick the Great, who is credited personally with increasing the population of Prussia by almost a third during his lifetime. Rousseau wished only to unchain the normal savage.

Locke taught that Life was a Fabula Rasa.

In the eighteenth century such greats as Mozart, Bach, Richardson, Roccoco, and Baroque cultured the nobles of Europe. Art was required to show harmony and trajectory. The modern piano replaced the clavicle as instrument of choice. *Don Giovanni* was Mozart's opera about Don Won.

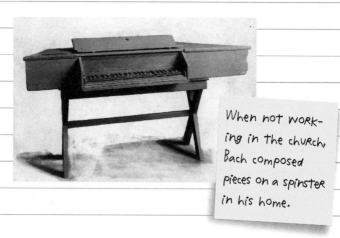

When not working in the church, Bach composed pieces on a spinster in his home.

Chapter 14
THE AGE OF REVOLUTION:
The French Demand Fraternities

Revolters demanded Liberty, equality and Fraternities

Another problem was that France was full of French people.

The American colonists lived on a continent and England was an island. Thus the Americans wanted independence.

Americans, of course, wanted no involvement in the French and Indian War because they did not want to fight in India. This led to the Stamp Act, where no stamps could be issued unless they bore the American mascot.

Tea formed a large surplice. The Boston Tea Party was held at Pearl Harbor. The Quebec Act was an Intolerable Act because it would have required Americans to learn French in school.

Surplice of tea

Another final straw in the camel's pack was when Britan tried to bar colonists from crossing the Appelation Mountains. Many Colonists became convicted patriots after reading *Horse Sense* by the escaped Englishman Thomas Pain.

The Americans had to mustard an army. Benjamin Franklin, already famous as inventor of the light bulb, persuaded French King George III to help the USA. The use of Haitian troups by the British violated the rites of Englishmen everywhere.

Yorktown was sight of Robert E. Lee's greatest victory. Washington defeated the Allies at Gettysberg. He was the first and only president to be elected anonymously by the Electoral College. Thomas Jefferson was president, founder of the University of Virginia, and author of the Decoration of Independence.

France was in a very serious state. Taxation was a great drain on the state budget.

Another problem was that France was full of French people. Dickens made this point in *The Tail of Two Sisters*, which he required us to read.

The French Revolution was like a tractor. It gave people the understanding that you need change in order to make tracks in the world. The Third Estate was locked out of its motel and had to do its business on a tennis court. This led to the Tennis Court Oath. This act of small deviance was the fuse that led to the explosion that blew up the government.

Revolters demanded liberty, equality, and fraternities. Fraternity breeded pride in the nation and therefore thicker political boundaries. Victims of the terror were rolled to

the gilotine in tumblers, an
unpleasant thing for all involved.
Many of these unfortunate people
became known as Emma Grays.

Along came a man named Robisieu
Thermidorean who saved the people.
The revolution evolved through monar-
chial, republican, and tolarian phases
until Napolean performed a coo in
1799. Napoleon was ill with blad-
der problems and was very
tense and unrestrained. As his
power leaked away his body
became a symbol. He was later
troubled by Spanish gorillas,
who formed a sore in his side.

Napoleon
fertilized all
his life. His
only son died
by a sphere.

The British defeated the
French from 1793 to 1815,
but at gastronomic cost.

Spinning Jenny was a young girl forced to work more than 40 hours a day.

the airplane was invented and first flown by the Marx brothers.

Chapter 15
THE INDUSTRIAL REVOLUTION:
The Fast Paste of Change

The industrial revolution was slow at first due to the lack of factories. European nations had the raw materials to start an industrial revolution, but they did not have the knowledge to start a revolution and thus they were retarded.

Robert Owen, for example, tried to set up a text tile plant. Later he became his own factory. Throughout the comparatively radical years 1815–1870 the western European continent was undergoing a Rampant Period of economic modification. The first example of a modification was in small cities such as Connecticut. Britain was the forerunner with France taking up the behind.

The Russians financed industrialization by selling bongs to foreign countries. Great progress was made through the introduction of self-acting mules. Thus technology helped the society to become more explosive.

An example of the importance of women during the industrial revolution was the work of Spinning Jenny, a young girl forced to work more than 40 hours a day.

Telephones were not available—communication went by mouth to mouth or telegram. The Interstate Highway System was built soon after the Civil War. The Trans-Siberian Railroad connected Europe to California. Urban mass transet included subways and electric tramps. The airplane was invented and first flown by the Marx brothers. Burt Einstein developed the theory of relativism.

Marie Curie won the Noel prize for inventing the Radiator.

Europe was disrupted by the fast paste of change. Industrialization was precipitating in England.

The social structure was Upper Class, Middle Class, Working Class, and Lowest Poor Scum.

• British paternalists were motivated by "noblesse oblique."

- **Successful businessmen could be raised to the porridge.**
- **Nobles claimed to be descended from better jeans.**

The old order could see the lid holding down new ideas beginning to shake. The middle class was tired and needed a rest. Certain members of the lower middle class exhibited boudoir pretensions.

By popular demand the U.S. Congress began the job of tryst-busting. Factory owners often treated their workers with condensation. The slums became brooding grounds for lower class unrest.

Poor street children often lived from foot to mouth as rat pickers.

Prostitution, considered to be the world's oldest profession, got its beginnings in the nineteenth century. At the bottom rung of the social spectrum was the **"lumpkin proletariate."**

In 1848, unemployment became a crisis in Paris. Out of a city population of one million people, two million able bodies were on the loose.

This was called the Roamantic Age, because everybody moved around. Moving and shaking grew more frequent. Villages in Europe could number from one up to a million people, but fear of diseases prevented people from wanting to come together.

The Irish had to imagrate to the United States because of Hitler.

Immigrants were packed into New York slums where living space and privates were scarce. This was the Gelded Age.

Nineteenth-century women wore frilly hats day in and day out unless they had a special activity to engage in. Middle class husbands had to be the sole breadmakers while their wives were placed on golden pesticules.

The law, however, treated women the same as children, criminals, or insominacs.

Girls were typically sent to finishing schools, where the point was to finish them off.

In 1887 and surrounding years it was unheard of to openly express yourself in private. Sex in this period was a very quiet ordeal.

Sigmund Freud was a shrink who came up with sex reasoning. He said that if the mind says not to have sex and the will will not listen, then the mind will go crazy. Leaders of the women's movement included Florence Nightengail, Susan B. Anthony, and Crystal Pancake. German feminists furthered the whatnot of women. Sufferance was the major goal.

Feminists aRgued that sex outside the Family would make you go blind oR lose youR memoRy.

In 1911 an English feminist attracted attention by plunging under the King's ascot.

Inspired by these ideas, reformers tried to ban sweating from the shops.

Chapter 16

POLITICAL CONFLICT IN THE NINETEENTH CENTURY:
Anarchs and the Power Serge

Metternich helped orcastrate the Concert of Europe. Great Brittian, the USA, and other countrys had demicratic leanings.

- **Liberals insisted on a lily fair economy, where it was hands off the lily.**
- **Among the goals of the chartists were universal suferage and an anal parliment.**
- **Voting was to be done by ballad.**

John Stuart Mill advocated total legal parody. In Russia the Decembrists attempted a coup du jour.

Bonapartism was the way of people that wanted Napoleon back to rule even though he was dead. The French revolution of 1848 happened mostly because Louis Philippe had become an annoying bore under the saddle of progress. Mazzini was a conservative liberal socialist who founded a revolutionary group known as "Little Italy."

Pope Leo XIII is known as the author of _Rectum Novarum_, a book of conservative ideas. He was hard-headed, pigmatic, and determined.

• Workers voted for conservatives, because they believed in unemployment.

- **Inspired by these ideas, reformers tried to ban sweating from the shops.**
- **The so-called "Great Reforms" of Alexander II included local government and the emaciation of the peasants. Neither was very successful.**

Newton and Darwin jumped out of the woodwork. Social Darwinism took place because of an internationally famous poet named James Darwin. No one could get enough of him.

Socialism advocates such views as: people choosing their own leaders, running their own businesses, freedom of speech, social assistance, and Family Allowances. Some people with socialist ideas are Edmund Burke and Prince Constantine. Big Bill Haywood was leader of the "Warblers," a socialist group.

Another man to influence the state and others was Karl Marx, who advanced his theory of dialectical maternalism. His ideas about revolution, condos, and supermen intrigued many. According to Marx the stages of history are canabalism, slavery, fuedalism, capitalism, and back to canabalism. These are the moods of production.

Karl Marx and his diabolical materialism

Flaming Anachronist Bakunin

Anarcho-cyclicalists were socialists who could not bring themselves to believe in Marx. Bakunin was a flaming anachronist. Anarchism is a system

of government headed by an Anarch.
Canada, for example, became an
anarchy in 1867.

A new time zone of national
unification roared over the horizon.
Founder of the new Italy was Cavour,
an intelligent Sardine from the north.
Nationalism aided Italy because
nationalism is the growth of an army.
We can see that nationalism succeeded
for Itally because of France's big
army. Prussia's army was also well-
brained.

Napoleon III-IV mounted the
French thrown. One thinks of
Napoleon III as a live extension of
the late, but great, Napoleon.

William I, the first Geyser of Germany

Here too was the new Germany: loud, bold, vulgar, and full of reality. German unity was acheaved by William I coupling with Bismark. After several hurtful convulsions he culminated to power as the first Geyser of Germany.

The Automaton Empire remained on the "Sick Bed of Europe" during this time.

Chapter 17

AMERICA FROM CRISIS TO TRIUMPH:
Custard's Last Stand

FLoRence Nightingale was a singeR who became involved with The AmeRican Flag.

Nineteenth-century America was an unequal society where only White males could download access to the power serge.

The Nullification Crisis was caused when Thomas Jefferson placed a tax on cotton gin. This greatly upset the South Carolinians.

John Quincy Adams was discovered outside himself after the 1828 election. Florence Nightingale was a singer who became involved with the American flag.

- **The major cause of the Civil War is when slavery spread its ugly testicles across the West.**
- **A factor in this was the Dead Scot decision. This case made a bang in President Buckanon.**
- **The Civil War began in 1830. Many soldiers repeatedly gave their lives for their country.**
- **The Confederates were greatly damaged by navel blockage.**

The First arcades were Fired at Fort Sumner.

Sherman launched his infamous "March to See." William McKinley was President of the South. Andrew Johnson was a knowledgable constrictionist. United States Grant was a Civil War heroe who later proved corrupulent as President. He died after drinking up to twenty cigars a day.

More pork barnacles were distributed than was actually a good idea. Grover Cleveland became the only U.S. President to serve two non-executive terms. Westward expansion ended at Custard's Last Stand and his later defeat at Wounded Knee.

Custard's Last Stand

This was the final result of "Man as Fist Destiny," an important motivational idea during the 1800s.

Oscar Wilde was probably the riskiest personage in England at this time.

Chapter 18

THE BIRTH OF MODERNISM:
Splatterism and the Twelve-Moan Scale

Culture fomented from Europe's tip to its top. Art plopped off the deep end and sailed up the creek without a paddle. Cubism, splatterism, etc. became the rage.

Picasso was the famous artist who painted the Mona Lisa. Benito Mussolini was an artist who became overly famous.

Seurat was the founder of pontificalism in painting.

Music reeked with reality. People did not forget Wagner's contribution. When he died they labeled his seat "historical."

Richard Strauss, who was violent but methodical like his wife made him, plunged into vicious and perverse plays. Another probably German composer expearmented with the twelve-moan scale.

- **Literature ran wild. Writers expressed themselves with cymbals.**
- ***George Eliot* was written by Silas Marner. This was the *nom de aplomb* of an English woman author.**
- **Oscar Wilde, the author of *Doreen Gray*, was probably the riskiest personage in England at this time.**

Other countries had their own artists. France had Chekhov. Dramatized were adventures in seduction and abortion. Many were

Bonjour marriage is ridaculed in Ibsen's play <u>A Doll's House,</u> where Torvald would deprive Nora of certain sweets such as mackerels.

conscious-stricken over such. The emergence of film gave artists a new median. Silent movies were already out of fashion before 1850.

Silent movie

Friedrich Nietzsche was a German movie producer who wrote *Triumph of the Will* and *Superman*.

There was a change in social morays. A new generation tittered on the brink of the end of an era.

Most English believed in the mission-ary position.

Chapter 19

IMPERIALISM AND INTERNATIONAL RIVALRIES:
From the Missionary Position to Sweet Relief

Imperialism was larger in the late ninetieth century. European countries were growing dramatically and instead of spilling onto each other they had to go elsewhere.

Another reason that the governments of European nations tried to take over other lands was so that they could gain so-called "cleavage."

According to George Orwell, the British reduced Burma to a small city north of India. Europeans in India inhabited designated spots where they could practice their imperialist values on one another. Another example of this is Rudward Kissinger's poem "The White Man's Burden."

The British practice imperialist values

- **Children born to Europeans and Asians were known as Euthanasians—a situation which troubled them for life.**
- **The "Arrow Insident" was when a British officer was slapped across the face by an Egyptian member.**

• General Gordon, a celibate who showed an interest in boys and visiting slums, involved himself in unusual mystical beliefs.

Thus the imperialist nations attempted to spread their ideals on the natives. Kitchener defeated an Arab leader known as the Mad He. Japan became a European country during the Benji Restoration. China, which was already weakened by imperialist spears of influence, produced the Boxcar Rebellion.

Lord Kitchener

The Russo-Japanese War exploded between Japan and Italy. Infestations of gold in South Africa led to the Boar War between England and Denmark.

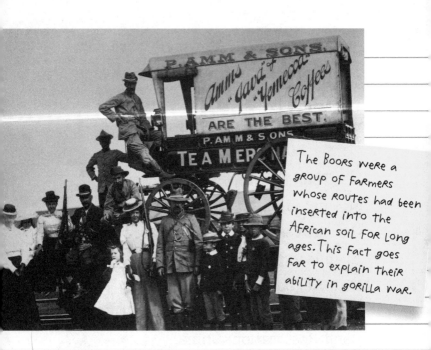

The Boors were a group of farmers whose routes had been inserted into the African soil for long ages. This fact goes far to explain their ability in gorilla war.

In 1898 the Spanish-American War was fought between the United States and Mexico. It gave rise to American generals such as Robert T. Lee and proved itself a highly useful war.

Admiral Dewey sank the Spanish Armada in Vanilla Bay.

Teddy ("J.R.") Roseaveld spoke softly, threatened with his big stick, and built the Panema Canal through Mexico. From this the events moved to an ensurpation by Poncho Vidalia.

Teddy ("J.R.") Roseaveld

Germany's William II had a chimp on his shoulder and therefore had to ride his horse with only one hand. The Austro-Hungarian Compromise was the result of a defeated Austria combing with Hungary. This was very strange.

Auto von Bismarck kept both sides from the middle. Archduke Rudolph used a suicide pack to kill himself and his girlfriend. This cleared the way to power for the young Francais Ferdinand.

- **All during this time Austria-Hungary was weakened by its problem of ethical diversity.**
- **The German takeover of All-Sauce Lorrain enraged the French, who clamored for vendetta.**

Dreyfus was a Frenchman who sold technicians to the Germans for money. The Drey-Fus chase was the biggest crises of all during this time. Lloyd George ran for office on the popular slogan *"soak up the rich."*

The Russian revolution of 1905 began about 1907. Unfortunately, the Czar was easily influenced by flutterers. The Triple

Alliance faced NATO. This too was
produced by Bismarck, who worked
for Caesar at the time.

The five European grade powers
were England, France, Germany,
Russia, and Australia-Mongolia.
Europe grew fevered with heated
tensions thrusting toward an outlet.
The Bland Hand Society in Sarajevo
caked the streets looking for the aire
to the throne.

In 1914 the assignation of
Archduke Ferdman gave sweet
relief to the mounting tensions.

Archduke
Ferdman

Rasputin was
a pheasant
by birth and
showed it in
his looks.

Men on both sides would have gotten to know each other much better if they didn't have to wear uniforms.

Chapter 20

THE CATASTROPHE OF 1914:

An Unthinkable War Becomes Thinkable

World War I broke out around
1912–1914. The deception of countries
to have war and those who didn't
want one led the countries of Europe
and the world to an unthinkable war
which became thinkable.

Germany was
on one side of
France and
Russia was on
the other.

The Germans used the "Schleppen Plan" to surprise France by attacking through Bulgaria, which is not far from Paris.

General von Falkenhayn, of course, was right: the French would breed themselves to death in order to retake Verdun. Many, however, died ineffectively.

Austria fought the Snerbs. The Allies versed the Turks. The British used mostly Aztec troops to fight at Gallipoli. Italy joined the Allies and this was useful because of their common border with Australia.

Aztecs land at Gallipoli

The Easter Indiscretion could be considered an expression of Irish feelings toward the war. Florence of Arabia fought over the dessert. At a certain point the British government began to grow weary of women's role in the war.

Florence of Arabia

The New White Star Liner, R.M.S. "TITANIC"

Unresurrected submarine warfare led the Germans to sink the Titanic and thus bring the USA into the war.

Military technology progressed with ideas such as guns which would shoot generally straight. At war people get killed, and then they aren't people anymore, but friends. After fighting in the trenches, the soldiers became close, no matter what their social standards. Men on both sides would have gotten to know each other much better if they didn't have to wear uniforms. When peace broke out the men excitedly relieved themselves wherever they were.

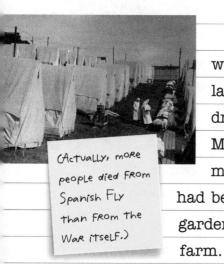

(Actually, more people died from Spanish Flu than from the War itself.)

Many of the war's causalities later came home to drain their familys. More than nine million young men had been led down the garden path to bite the farm.

It is hard to believe that all who took part in the war were first cousins, but stranger things have happened. I guess.

Chapter 21
THE RUSSIAN REVOLUTION:
Rasputin Meets the Zeitgeist

Russia's chances in this war were largely farfetchual. Tsarist Russia was poor and backward despite government efforts to encourage the military-industrial complex and space technology.

Nicholas II Let himself be pulled into strainful positions by his wife.

The Russian middle class were called Bolsheviks.

Communism raged among the peasants.

Nicholas II let himself be pulled into strainful positions by his wife. To make matters worse, his son was diagnosed with hemophilatelism, a sickness which required him to fall down and hurt himself badly.

Rasputin made friends with the Zeitgeist. Russian generals were idiots and Russian industry could only produce one or two bullets every year. The army, no surprise, soon was destestimated.

The only choice for Russian soldiers was to use their guns as spheres.

All this and more was predicted
by Lenin in *Capitalism: The Highest
Stage of Socialism.*

Lenin rose to power by promising
"Peace, Land and Reds."
The civil war "team
colours" were red and
white. Trotsky hoped only
for a military insertion.
Meanwhile, all the
Liberals could do was to
try to give a goat to
democracy.

In 1937 Lenin
Revolted Russia
after the
Germans sent
him home on a
soiled train.

**Nearly everybody breathed a
sigh of relief when the Communists
were able to restore chaos.**

Cat berets were a favorite form of German entertainment at this time.

Chapter 22

THE INTER-WAR ERA:
Just Give Peas a Chance

Peace was proclaimed at Versigh, which was attended by George Loid, Primal Minister of England. President Wilson arrived with fourteen pointers. When Woodrow Wilson suffered a stroke, the head cheerleader for the League of Nations lost his pompoms.

El Alamein was an Indian leader who sent his son Faisal to the conference. Germany was displaced after World War I. The Treaty of Trianon cost Hungary more than six fifths of its land. Austria and Turkey were left to wander by themselves.

Many people got new countries who shouldn't have. After the war the great powers tried to cut military spending by building enormous navies.

Germany was morbidly excited and unbalanced. The Wiener Republic was nobody's ticket to democracy. Berlin became the decadent capital, where all forms of sexual deprivations were practised.

- **The Beer Hall Putsch was a popular lesbian on the large scale.**
- **Cat berets were a favorite form of German entertainment at this time.**
- **The Spartacist revolt was led by a man and woman named Rosa Luxemburg.**

The United States experienced a Red scarce shortly after World War I.

Economic problems were caused mostly by falling prices, a problem we now recognize as inflation.

The Teapot Doom scandal was a factor leading to Prohibition.

J. M. Keynes tells us there is no existence between big government and business. When the Davy Jones Index crashed in 1929 many people were left to political incineration. Some, like John Paul Sart, retreated into extra-terrestrialism. Bad economic conditions led militarists to pull off coops in several countries. The New Deal was an idea inspired by President Franklin Eleanor Roosevelt.

Wall St. panics as Davy Jones crashes

Lennon ruled in Russia. He was first zar of the Soviet Union. Eventually he started the NOPE (No Economic Plan) to encourage the peasants. When he died the USSR was run by a five man triumpherate—Stalin, Lenin, Trotsky, Menshevik, and Buchanan.

Stalin expanded capitalism by building machine tractor stations. Workers who exceeded their quotas were placed above others as stalactites. Stalin wrote *Dizzy with Success* to justify his refrigeration of the kulaks.

When things didn't go as planned, Stalin used the peasants as escape goats.

A huge anti-semantic movement arose. This attitude encouraged the German people to embrace Hitler's raciest ideas and plans for the Third Reich. Hitler, of course, wanted to become the only race.

- **Military leaders helped put Hitler in power by forming a cahoots with him.**
- **The night of glass took place when Hitler ordered Nazis to smash all windows. Fearocity was key to his sucess.**

As Nazi leader of a Communist Germany, Hitler was one leader who wanted all for himself and none for all.

Totalitarianism subjects its citizens to ruthless propagation. Stalin and Hitler were influential and highly viscous leaders who changed the course of history.

Hitler's instrumentality of terror was the Gespach

- **Citizens were often enlightened with lies.**

- **As Hitler said, *"you can fool all of the people all of the time and some of the people from time to time."***

- **The bigger the whooper the more it had believablness.**

• These mass propaganda pogroms are perhaps best captivated by Adolph Huxley in his novel *1984*.

Hitler re-militarized the Rineland over a squirmish between Germany and France. Nazi Germany and Italy agreed to the Pact of Steal. Thus was formed the alliance between the Anxious Powers.

Hitler believed in a Panned Germany and therefore insisted that Czechoslavia release the Sedated Germans into his care. Later he acquired them after making a deal with Munich.

In Spain Franco performed a Falange. England's rulers vanely hoped for ***"peas in our time,"*** but were completely foddled by Hitler.

Moosealini Rested his Foundations on eight million boyonets and invaded Hi Lee Salasy.

President of England at this time was Nebble Chamberman, who appeared in videos as a man with a boulder hat. The appeasers were blinded by the great red light of the Soviets.

The policy of appeasement might have worked, however, if it was not for Hitler.

Chapter 23

WORLD WAR II:
Hitler Becomes Depressed

Japan boomed Pearl Harbor, the main U.S. base in southern California.

Few were surprised when the National League failed to prevent another world war. The perverbial chickens laid by the poor peace treaties after World War I all came home to roast.

The situation before 1939 had all the ingredients to bake a perfect war. Stalin and Hitler used the Molotov Ribbon Drop Pack to divide Eastern Europe on the eave of the war.

Germany invaded Poland, France invaded Belgium, and Russia invaded everybody.

The Germans took the by-pass around France's Marginal Line. This was known as the **"Blintz Krieg."** The French huddled up and threw sneers at the Germans. Japan boomed Pearl Harbor, the main U.S. base in southern California. American sailors watched in shock as the sky filled with Japanese zebras.

Soviets resist Operation Barbarella

Hitler's attack on Russia was secretly called "Operation Barbarella." The German invaders were popular for a while in Russia, but their habit of slaughtering innocent civilians tended to give them an image problem. The Russians defended Stalingrad feercely, as the city was named after Lenin.

The Allies landed near Italy's toe and gradually advanced up her leg, where they hoped to find Musalini.

Casualties sprouted on both sides. Billions died. Stalin carefully set his bead on Germany. After a time Charles DiGaul started a group called "Let's Free France."

Hitler, who had become depressed for some reason, crawled under Berlin. Here he had his wife Evita put to sleep, and then shot himself in the bonker.

Unfortunately, the Second World War was not concluded until 1957. A whole generation had been wiped out in two world wars, and their forlorne families were left to pick up the peaces.

WaR scReeched to an end when a nuKuLeeR expLosion was dRopped on HeRoshima.

Martin Luther Junior's famous "If I Had a Hammer" speech.

Chapter 24

THE COLD WAR:
The Morels of the Story

World War II became the Cold War, because Benjamin Franklin Roosevelt did not trust Lenin and Stalin. An ironed curtin fell across the haunches of Europe.

The ball of events and stoppers that were used to stop it from rolling only added to its momentum which kept it rolling.

BeRLin was aiRLifted westwaRd and divided into pieces.

Poland migrated toward the Atlantic Ocean.

The Marsha Plan put Europe back together with help from Konrad Adenauer, a French leader whose efforts led to the Communist Market. Many countries signed the GNAT Agreement.

- **The USSR and USA became global in power, but Europe remained incontinent.**
- **Israel was founded despite the protests of local Arabs known as Zionists.**

• In 1956 the United States became distracted by the Sousa Crisis.

The Russians invaded Poland to show the revolting Hungarians what was what.

Wars fought in the 1950s and after include the Crimean War, Vietnam, and the Six-Minute War. President Eisenhower resorted to the bully pool pit. John F. Kennedy

worked closely with the Russians to solve the Canadian Missile Crisis.

The Canadian Missile Crisis

The Berlin Wall was built some-where in Europe. President Kennedy soothed the masses, however, with his story about *"Itch Ben the Berliner."*

Yugoslavia's Toto became a non-eventualist communist. Hochise Min mounted the power curve in Viet Nam. Korea became a peninsula. Chairman Moo tried to forclothes all outside ideas in China.

Castro led a coupe in Cuba and shocked many by wiggling his feelers every time there was trouble in Latin America.

This required the United States to middle in selected bandana republics during the 1960s.

The British Empire has entered a state of recline. Its colonies have slowly dribbled away leaving only the odd speck on the map.

Mohammed Gandi, for example, was the last British ruler of India. Gandhi became famous for using peace as a weapon. This was a good way to get through to people.

In 1921 Gandi cast off his western clothes and dawned a loin cloth.

The French Empire, on the other hand, fell into total term-oil as they clutched painfully at remaining colonies in Argentina and the Far East.

South Africa followed "Apart Hide," a policy that separated people by skin colour.

Actually, the fall of empires has been a good thing, because it gives more people a chance to exploit their own people without outside interference.

The Civil Rights movement in the USA turned around the corner with Martin Luther Junior's famous "If I Had a Hammer" speech. Martian Luther King's four steps to direct action included self purification, when you allow yourself to be eaten to a pulp. The wealing and dealing of President Lynda B. Johnson was another important factor.

Lynda B. Johnson

Richard Nixon felt free to shed his morels after defeating Hubert Hoover. The roll of women has greatly

expanded also. Famous women since
the Second World War are Queen
Victoria and India Gandy.

Mentally speaking, Russia had to
reinvent itself. After Stalin died there
was an interogation that lasted three
years as Krushev criticized Stalin for
indiscretions like slaughtering the
kulaks. This introduced many
western policies to Russia, such as
the use of strippers at clubs.

A graph of Nikita Khrushchev's
life would appear to be the blueprint of
a stomach-turning roller coaster resulting from what can be called a meta-
morphosis. One of his least successful
ideas was the "Virgin Soil" programme,
where milk and butter were expected
to grow in unusual places.

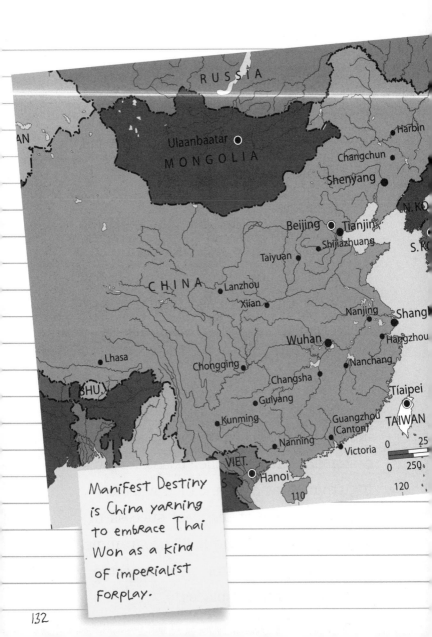

Manifest Destiny is China yarning to embrace Thai Won as a kind of imperialist forplay.

Chapter 25

A NEW WORLD ORDER:
Tea with Dim El Sum

History grundled onward.
International relationships moved to
the broodle stage.

Gorbachev became top Russian
after the death of Leoned Bolshevik.
Gradually the USSR shifted to a new
planet of existance.

East and West made mends with
each other. The Berlin
Mall was removed.
Many Eastern Europeans
experienced a new form
of arousal at this time.

The Berlin Mall

The Balkens returned as a powdered keg. Rumaina's Chou Tse Cu was deplaced from his pedisal. Yugoslavia moved toward the edge of its end, trebled and plunged into the bowels of deconstruction.

North Africa is the region which lies in the northern part of Africa. It is therefore not in Africa. Without a dout this was the Middle East, where all bets were misplaced. Arab leaders ran head in tail with the Soviets.

One major source of conflict since World War II has been Israel's relations with the Parisians. The Carter administration found itself face to face with this problem during the so-called Iran Hostess Crisis.

Dim El Sum ruled as "Head Coucho" of North Korea. China had so many Chinese that forced birth patrol became required. This is where people are allowed to reproduce no more than one half of themselves. Manifest Destiny is China yarning to embrace Thai Won as a kind of imperialist forplay.

Birth patrol poster

- **"Third World" is a eulogism for undeveloped nations.**
- **One index of this situation is a poor infant morality rate.**
- **Another problem is lack of practise with self-rain.**

Sub-Sonora Africa still counts many people treated like second hand citizens.

Corruption grew especially ripe in Zaire, where Mobutu was  known to indulge in more than an occaisonal little armadillo.

The plurious of wealth was therefore uneven. The rural populus was reduced to tenement farming. It is also little help that former colonialists continue to watch events with sharp ears.

Thus the pedestrians of the rich countries should listen to their conscious more often. This would make the possibility of better times less of a pipe steam.

Chapter 26
THE END OF HISTORY:
The Age of Now

Planets now ROLL against incredible odds of chance.

The historicle period ended shortly after World War II–III. Historians and others attempt to pin the tail on the reluctant monkey of change.

The public appears no brighter than a herd of lemmings spreading toward a cliff. Thus has our stream of consciousness developed a waterfall.

There has been a change of social seen. The last stage is us. We, in all humidity, are the people of currant times.

It is now the age of now. This concept grinds our critical, seething minds to a halt.

POSTSCRIPT

The Meaning of All This

At the very least this excursion into the past should disabuse anyone of the silly notion that history is stuffy and boring. Does it send any deeper message? Is it disturbing evidence of a generation raised in ignorance by incompetent schools and disengaged parents? Should we sound the alarms and, in imitation of the late Joseph Stalin, grab some handy "escape goats"? Maybe.

What really lies behind these flights of creative inanity? One source is the mistaken and dangerous assumption that spell-check programs perform a proofreading service. The anxieties and time constraints of taking exams can also produce devastating results. Exam blue books are littered with mind-numbing absurdities from students who (one hopes) must know better. What else can possibly explain how four statesmen of the World War II era came to be known as the "Big Three"?

On the other hand, precious little can be taken for granted about the historical knowledge (not to mention the language skills) that freshmen bring to college. It is probably safe to assume that every American college freshman knows the following:

1. At some point in the distant past the United States fought a war of independence against a major European or Asian power. An extraordinary Tea Party was a factor.

2. George Washington, Abraham Lincoln, John Kennedy, and Richard Nixon served as presidents of the United States. Washington was the first president and Lincoln also lived a long time ago, while the latter two were in the twentieth century. Ronald Reagan and George Bush the First were more recent occupants of the Oval Office. (Jimmy Carter is already off the radar screen for more than a few young scholars of the 2000s.)

3. The United States still suffers from the horrors of its slaveholding past, whenever that was. The Civil War, which took place some time between 1750 and 1930, was mixed up with this.

4. Adolf Hitler (a foreigner of some kind) was a very bad man.

5. There was at least one World War, but absolutely not more than three.

Beyond this the ground becomes very shaky. For Canadians the knowledge base has similar depth, but somewhat different content. The American Civil War might be an iffy proposition, but all of them would certainly recognize Sir John A. MacDonald as a highly important, if deceased, prime minister. (His appearance on the ten dollar bill helps.)

The geography situation is even scarier. More than a few college freshmen cannot even locate their own home towns on a map of their state or province. (See maps, pages 146–150.) Another common problem is confusing Mexico with Spain. In an effort to plumb these depths I once gave a brief geography quiz to a class of forty freshmen. About a third knew that Dublin was in Ireland. Other answers included England, China, France, South Africa, Boston, and Chicago. We can only hope that these people are not shy about asking for directions.

A World History or Western Civilization course can be a daunting swirl of unfamiliar ideas, names, places, and events for those who start from near ground zero. It's so easy to get them all jumbled. Add to this a dose of distracted note taking, last-minute cramming, and limited vocabulary. The result is the kind of bizarre free associations that have Roman senators exchanging togas for tubas, Caesar perishing on the Yikes of March, and monotheism originating with a God named Yahoo.

Does the current generation of young North American scholars have a monopoly on imaginative historical revisionism? Probably not. To err, sometimes with hilarious results, is a feature of the human condition. Some of the material in this collection was written in the early 1970s by the parents of today's students. W. C. Sellar and R. J. Yeatman's wonderful classic *1066 and All That** satirized student prose at elite British schools during the 1920s, when all those chaps could quote Shakespeare and conjugate irregular Latin verbs. And who knows what madcap observations Aristotle found on the exam tablets of Alexander the Great?

*W. C. Sellar and R. J. Yeatman, *1066 and All That* (London: Methuen, 1930).

Quiz:

So You Think You're So Smart

A re students the only manglers of history? How historically literate are we who chuckle over their amusing malapropisms? The following quiz, self-administered in complete privacy, might be revealing. These questions test information that college freshmen would be expected to know upon completion of a World History 101 survey course. How do you score?

1. In what decade(s) did the following occur?

_____ Boxer Rebellion

_____ Balfour Declaration

_____ Boer War

_____ Unification of Italy

_____ Meiji Restoration

_____ Crimean War

_____ Congress of Vienna

_____ Cuban Missile Crisis

2. During which century did the following live?

_____ Cleopatra

_____ Charlemagne

_____ Constantine

_____ Mohammed

_____ Martin Luther

_____ Confucius

3. Who are these people?

Mary Wollstonecraft

Ignatius Loyola

Sun Yat-sen

Hildegard of Bingen

Marcus Aurelius

Harun al-Rashid

Akhenaton

Chaka

Marie Curie

Hung-wu

Elijah

Oliver Cromwell

4. What do these terms mean?

Anarcho-syndicalism

Dialectical materialism

Predestination

Sophism

Cathar

Social Darwinism

Jacobin

Taoism

Sunnite

Maoism

Anabaptist

Hellenistic

Scoring: Totally private self-assessment. Choose one of the following:

A. *Piece of cake! What's the matter with kids today?*

B. *Never mind.*

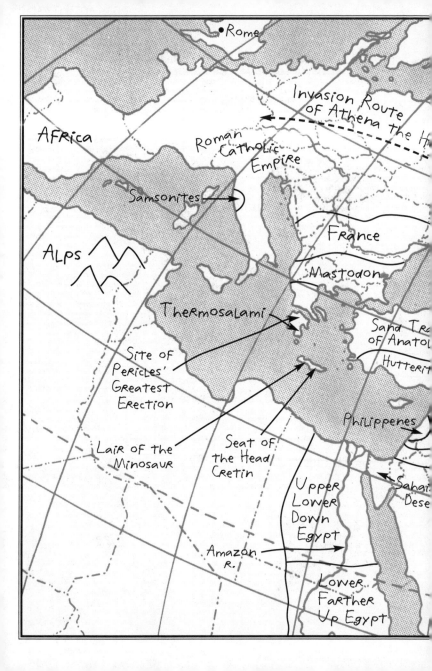

Visible Goths

Invisible Goths

Hungs

Zulus

Mt. Arafat

Home of Golden Fleas

Arcadia

Eucalyptus R.

Nile R.

Erotic Flooding Zone

Mongrels

Land of Milk and Chocolate

The Ancient World

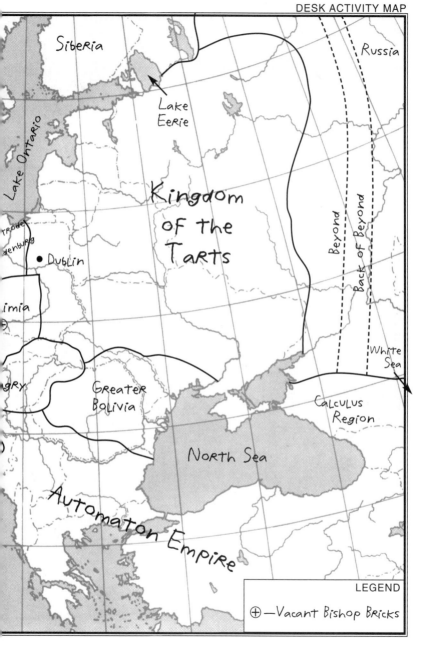

Siberia

Russia

Lake
Eerie

Lake Ontario

Kingdom
of the
Tarts

Beyond

Back of Beyond

Troder
denburg

Dublin

imia

White
Sea

gry

Greater
Bolivia

Calculus
Region

North Sea

Automaton Empire

LEGEND

⊕—Vacant Bishop Bricks

China

Korea

Antarctica

South Pole

England

Boston

New England

Siberia

BALTIC Sea

USSR

Moscow

Bermuda

Ireland

Manhattan

Japan

Atlanta

Washington

Long Island

Pearl Harbor

California

USA

Appellation Mts.

San Francisco

Chile

Granola

Cuba

Territory of Poncho Vidalia

Spain

West Indonesia

Panama Canal

British Columbia

Bandana Republics

America and Its Neighbors

EPILOGUE

Knowledge of the Middle East and the wider Islamic world has acquired a new-found relevance since this little volume first appeared. Names and places once considered exotic are now staple fare for the news media; and colleges across the continent have responded with programs designed to bring today's issues home to their students.

Are we all tuned in? A recent National Geographic Society survey of Americans aged 18 to 24 revealed that only one in seven could locate Iraq on a map. But the Society's survey included people of all educational backgrounds. Surely college students would perform better. Or would they? What follows is a portrait of Islam and recent Middle Eastern history in the students' own words. There is a handy map as well. Nearly all of the material has been harvested since the fall of 2001. I am again indebted to my friends and colleagues across North America, especially Pam Lange and Joe Beene.

Sandy Arabia and the Palaced Indians

Islam was founded around 1900. The Koran took place during the Tang Dynasty. Believers take the five pills of faith. Ramadan is the feast of fast-breaking. Hindus are Muslims from India. Sunnites believe in the sun. The Druze are an Islamic sex. Some are restrictualists and others

disagree. Women are very oppressed in Iran,

Every Moslem is encouraged to go to Mecca on a hydRangia.

Mosques are what the people are required to wear to church.

where they are forced to be in a chapati for all activities. The idea here is to keep them barefoot and childproof. Shiites are Islamic feminists.

The main problem in the Middle East today is that there are problems. There would not be all these problems if the West Bank would lend more money to the Arabs and if the Palaced Indians were not so troublesome. Many of the countries suffer rule by monocolism.

- **The Baathist Party stands for socialism and personal cleanliness.**
- **The P.L.O is the airline of Israel.**
- **Taliban is the language of Africa.**
- **The U.S. Secretary of State is Coleman Paul.**

The Iranian Revolution led to the power of Komoto as supreme one.

The Iran–Iraq War was fought in the nineteenth century between the Arabs and Israel. The Camp David Accords was when Reagan ended the Iran–Iroque War. Saddam Hussein is ruler of the Iraquois who used

the Pershing Gulf War began when Satan Husane invaided Kiwi and Sandy Arabia.

venomous gas and kamakazies against his own people. This was an act of premedication. An angry world proclaimed him to be abdominal.

We are glad that the Persian war ended with victory to the cotillion. Current cause for concern is the creeping of fomentalism among the people.

Pershing war tanks

This spells out the whole thing in a nuthouse.

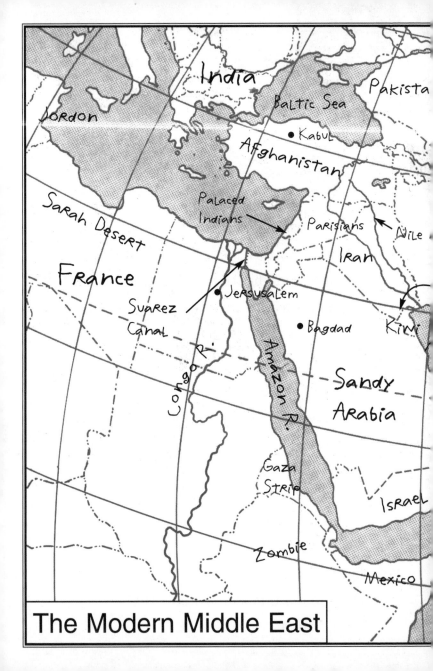

China

Cashmere

Japan

ia

Egypt

que

Somalia

Route
n Husane

Bangle Dangle

Nabob

GULF

um

Texas

GULF OF

Mexico

naica

• Cairo

Cuba

Praise for *Non Campus Mentis*

"The crème de la crème of student vacantness . . . Mangled vocabulary, inventive spelling, and historical blunders, it seems, are the stuff of bestsellers. Chuckles . . . have carried *Non Campus Mentis* onto *The New York Times* bestseller list."

—Vicki Smith, Associated Press

✻

"Shocking and hysterical. You'll laugh until you cry, shedding tears for the state of American education."

—*Baltimore Sun*

✻

"What endears these fragments of tortured prose to Henriksson is a bizarre species of higher truth that some contain. Who would quarrel today with the student who wrote: 'The fall of empires has been a good thing, because it gives more people a chance to exploit their own people without outside interference'?"

—Ken Ringle, *The Washington Post*

✻

"Call them malaprops, bloopers, or blunders. The compilation's display of ignorance is bliss to read—revisionist history with a vengeance."

—*Capital Times*, Madison, Wisconsin

✻

"Wading through this mass of malapropisms . . . provides occasion for thinking about how STDs—Sensorily Transmitted Dumbnesses—are caught by students, and what can be done about it."

—Knight-Ridder News Service